Upside Down

the poems and drawings
of C.G. Metz

ISBN-10: 1489578595
ISBN-13: 978-1489578594

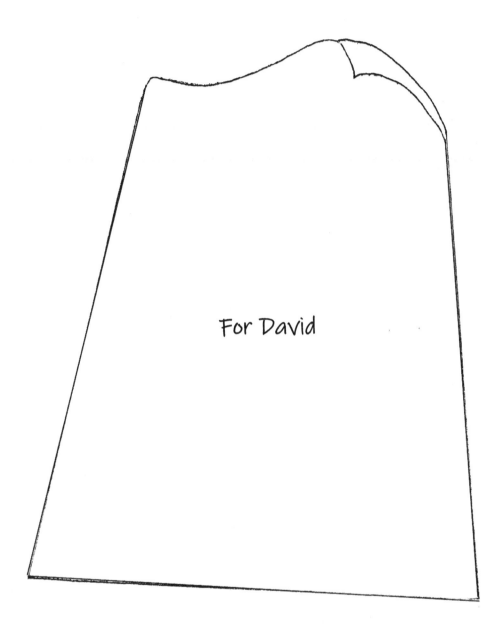

For David

ACKNOWLEDGMENTS

I would like to acknowledge Kevin for his patience and encouragement, and David for being the inspiration behind these poems.

COME INSIDE

Come inside, come inside…
And keep your mind open wide!
Discover where your dreams hide.
This is where your deepest wishes come true
And you'll find out what your mind can do.
Come inside to a place called YOU!

WORDS

If you could eat words
What would you eat?
Words that are bitter?
Or words that are sweet?
Maybe tart like sauerkraut
Would be more to your taste?
Or something fresh and minty,
Perhaps like toothpaste?
I would eat a lot of words…
But would be sure to use great care,
And I'd definitely avoid words
Like **toilet** and **underwear**!

Bugs

CRACKER

FRUIT

Cupcake

Pizza

Toilet

Dirty

cookie   Underwear

**Litter
Box**   **Tofu**

Tuna fish

Hot dog

Toot   **Chocolate**

Dog food   Cheese

Spinach   **Diaper**

Surprise

Taco

Candy

Sauerkraut   Roast Beef

vomit

DINOSAUR RODEO

Come old, and come small—
To the most exciting rodeo of all!
It's the year 2095 or thereabout—
And it's so far in the future science has figured out
How to make dinosaurs alive again,
And it's sure bringing the crowds in!
It's standing room only at every dinosaur rodeo show,
And the dinosaur cowboys are always raring to go!
But it's the dinosaurs the people are coming to see—
The big, the bad, and the awesome—don't you agree?
Raptor racing is always such a big hit,
And the bucking brachiosaurus is something you won't forget!
Feel the ground shake and hear the people shriek,
"Look at the length of that Pterodactyl's beak!"
Triceratops roping keeps you on the edge of your seat,
And you won't believe the size of the T-Rex's feet!
Dangerous—what's that you say?
No way, I haven't seen anyone eaten all day!

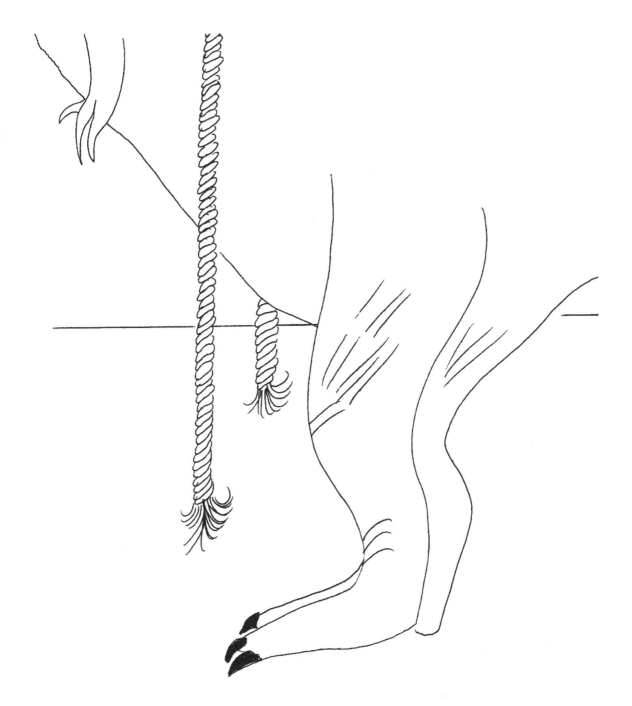

THE PITS!

I can handle my older brother's fits
And even his unfair hits!
The gross popping of his zits
And his filthy baseball mitts!
But nothing is worse than his stinky pits!

RATS

No brushing or combing,
No fixing my hair!
No grooming or braiding,
And barrettes I don't wear!
No fussing or straightening,
No pony tails at all!
No curling and crimping,
Or twisting my hair in a ball!
No shampooing or conditioning,
No hairspray please!
No cutting or trimming,
That makes me sneeze!
No touching or teasing,
No feeding them in there!
No pestering or playing with
The rats in my hair!

EWE MEET YOU

I'd like to introduce you to Ewe…
Doesn't she have soft fluffy hair?
You say you already know Ewe?
How did you meet her, and where?
She just said, "Baa, I don't know you?
Did you see me at the fair?"

STRIPES

The other day I came upon some black stripes
Just lying there on the ground.
I didn't know where it was,
Or I would have taken them to the lost and found.
But as luck would have it,
I ran into a white horse galloping past.
He saw the stripes I was holding,
And he said, "Oh, I found my stripes at last!"
"Although they are a little wrinkled,
I'm so thankful to you sir.
Now I'll need to find a way
To put my stripes back on the way they were."
So luckily I was able to find a paint roller,
And dipped the stripes in some special glue.
Then I rolled them gently on his body,
And before long he looked as good as new!
He was black and white,
And now had stripes from head to toe.
But then I noticed something and asked,
"Mr. Zebra, where did your tail go?"

CRUMBS

My brother ate some pretzels
And he snacked on cereal.
He scarfed down some crackers—
It looks like he had quite a meal!
He ate a few glazed donuts
And enjoyed potato chips.
He wolfed down a lot of cornbread,
Along with some chicken strips!
You ask me how I know this?
It's not from what he's said.
I've been trying to sleep all night
With this pile of crumbs in my bed!

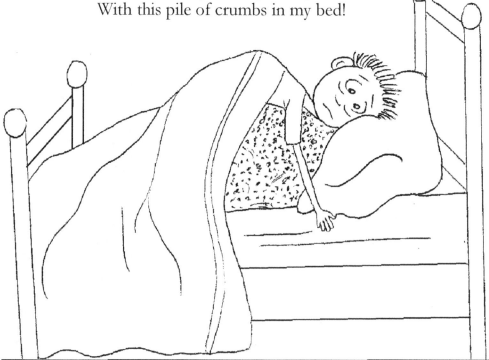

PETE THE PARAKEET

Pete was a very stubborn parakeet,
And would bob his head and stomp his feet.
He only said one thing when you tried to teach him a new word,
"Pretty bird, turkey bird, whatcha doin' turkey bird?"
And then he would ignore you and eat!
I'm not sure where Pete learned the phrase—
And it only took him a couple of days.
When my friends came over he would still act absurd—
All he said was, "Pretty bird, turkey bird, whatcha doin' turkey bird?"
And Pete never did change his ways!

BEAUREGARD THE BULL

Beauregard the bull's favorite color was red.
When all the other bulls couldn't stand it,
Beauregard loved that color instead.
When he saw red it made him feel happy inside,
But when his bull friends saw it…
They chased the people and made them run and hide!
Beauregard's love of red made him one of a kind.
People came from all over to see him,
Waving at him with anything red they could find.
But one day a man learned what really made him mean,
And it wasn't seeing the color red...
It was seeing the color green!

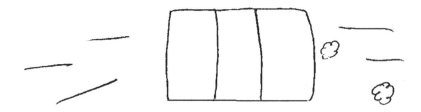

CHOPS

Chops is my brother's remote control helicopter,
And he's a terrifying sight!
Ever since he arrived last Christmas,
Our household has been living in fright!
One day Chops visited my poor kitty Fritz,
Who was the first to experience Chops' wrath.
Suddenly while Fritz was sleeping—
Chops picked him up for an unscheduled bath!
For that Chops was grounded for quite a long time,
And Fritz kitty will probably never be the same.
But after a month or so Chops was flying again,
Looking for another victim to claim!
Next on his list was my favorite baby doll—
Chops held her hostage one day.
He swooped in and got her off of my bed,
And he took her outside to play.

He dropped her in our flower garden,
And slugs made a mess of her hair.
I finally found her and rescued her,
But not before she got a tear!
After that mission Chops was grounded again,
But my baby doll doesn't look the same—
I had to sew her up with about seven stitches,
And Chops is the one to blame!
I'm tired of him terrorizing our house—
He's been hovering low for about a year.
And Fritz, baby doll, and I have finally decided
That we're not going to live in fear!
So this year my Santa list includes
The biggest remote control helicopter in town.
And if Chops feels the need to strike again…
My Chops Eater II will bring him down!

BUBBLE GUM

Bubble gum in the morning,
Bubble gum at night,
Bubble gum stretched out,
And holding together my kite.
Bubble gum on the ceiling,
Bubble gum on the floor,
Bubble gum on my fingers,
As I walk out the door.
Bubble gum you're getting sticky!
Bubble gum this isn't fair!
Bubble gum you're getting all over,
And now you're stuck in my hair!
Bubble gum I'm getting worried!
Bubble gum I thought you were my friend?
Bubble gum how can I chew you
When I'm wrapped up end–to–end?

PIRATE

I'm the fiercest pirate you ever did see!
This stick is my sword, and even the rain is afraid of me!
I've fought sheets of rain, and cut rain drops in half.
I've battled and conquered, and then let out my mighty pirate laugh!

Ho, ho, hum—I'm waiting for the rain to strike again.
I'm wearing my eye patch, because it helps me see to win.
I've found a bigger sword now, and I'm ready to go.
Excuse me—I just saw a raindrop on the window!

ARMY AUNT

Hut one, hut two, hut three, hut four—
My army aunt marched right through the door!
Hut five, hut six, hut seven, hut eight—
She just got back from some time in Kuwait.

She marched to the left and then to the right—
Found the spare room and said, "Goodnight."
But 0' five hundred came too soon…
My army aunt was up barking orders 'til noon!

"Clean your room and make your bed—
Shine those shoes," is what she said.
Then it was time for our five mile run.
She told me that's what she did for fun.

At dinner mom was told to make the slop,
And I was ordered to go and get the mop.
I cleaned the floor 'til it was spick and span,
While my dad scrubbed every pot and pan.

We did the same thing day–after–day,
Until finally it was time for her to go on her way.
She said, "I know you're sad I can't stay a day more,"
Then she marched out the door like she marched in before!

Since we last saw her it's been three hundred days,
And we've barely recovered from her military ways.
But we just learned she's coming to visit us again,
And we're busy cleaning now because inspection is at ten!

CORN ON THE COBB

It's funny when I smile
After I eat corn on the cobb.
My teeth are really yellow,
And my sister says I look like a slob!
Bits of corn are stuck everywhere—
All over my teeth and in between.
My parents cringe in their seats,
It's the grossest sight they've seen!
But I have something better in store,
And I can't wait to see their faces,
When I smile after eating corn on the cobb,
In my brand new braces!

THE DEEP DARK PIT

It's a deep dark pit!
It can swallow you up!
Filled with crumbs and gum wrappers,
Lipstick, loose change—
And once even a ripped up paper cup!
Receipts and broken pens—
Sometimes I put my hand in reverse!
It's scary and frightening—
When my mom asks me to…
Get something out of her purse!

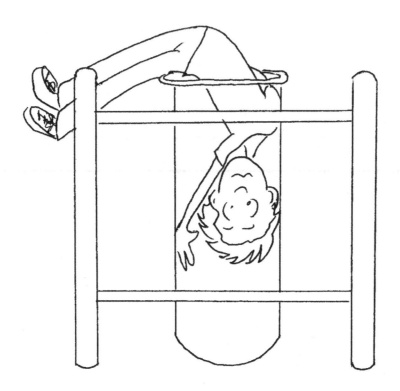

MY OWN SCIENCE EXPERIMENT

I'm my own science experiment—
I'm sure I'll get an A.
I'm searching for the biggest microscope,
And goggles and an extra-large tray.
Now I'm measuring myself onto a scale,
Then scooping me into a huge beaker.
I'm throwing in my dirty socks,
And my really smelly sneaker.
Then I'm squeezing myself into a giant test tube.
Oh no! I have to write down what I see!
There is one small problem with that—
How am I going to see me?

THE SCHOOL JOG-A-THON

It happened at the school jog-a-thon...
My mom and my little brother were there,
Cheering me on to my fourth lap around,
Then my brother started tugging at his underwear!
On my fifth lap around he was crossing his legs,
And by the sixth he was doing the potty dance.
My mom didn't notice until he shouted to me,
"Guess what? I just wet my pants!"

BUSTER

Buster, you chew too much—
Don't chew anymore!
No, Buster don't do that—
Don't chew on the door!

Oh no! You didn't do it…
Not mom's expensive shoes!
You know when she finds out about this,
It's going to be really bad news!

Buster, resist the urge to chew!
That's all I'm asking now.
Where is that stuffing coming from?
Don't tell me you chewed up my stuffed cow!

Come, Buster—let's play fetch,
And forget about chewing for a while!
Buster, you bad pooch, what did you do?
How did you get mom's nail file?

Where are you going?
Buster, go get your ball!
That's not where it is…
And what are you dragging down the hall?

No—not dad's slipper,
You'll be in a big trouble for that!
You've already gotten his electric razor,
And his nail clipper and his hat!

I have to do my homework now.
Where did my backpack go?
What's that hanging out of your mouth?
I think I'm afraid to know!

Yep, you got my homework!
Now what am I going to do?
The teacher won't believe it,
But this time it's really true!

PET STORE

The pet store is a dangerous place!
It's somewhere you shouldn't linger.
If you don't read the warning signs,
You could find a ferret dangling off of your finger!

KARAOKE

I can't stand it anymore
Please make it stop!
If my sister sings one more note
My ear drums will pop!
My poor dog is howling—
He's in agony and pain!
The high pitched singing
Is making us both go insane!
My stomach is churning!
My cat's hair is raised!
The earmuffs aren't helping,
And my lizard looks crazed!
I need to pull the plug fast!
Does my face look green?
I think I might barf all over…
My sister's new karaoke machine!

FRONT TOOTH

I lost my front tooth I'm here to say!
I lost my front tooth and its picture day!
Quick, I need a pistachio shell and some dental floss,
And then maybe nobody will notice my loss!
Oh no! That didn't work out too well—
Maybe if I put a mini marshmallow there no one could tell?
Where are the marshmallows…pictures are at ten?
Please don't tell me this marshmallow isn't staying in!
I'm racking my brain—it's already nine!
I'll just smile with my lower teeth and I'll be fine!
Does anyone have a mint I can borrow?
I promise I'll give it back tomorrow!

It didn't stick—now what do I do?
And it's already nine-thirty-two!
Panic has set in and I'm feeling numb.
I wonder if I can find a wad of gum?
That's right there's no gum at school.
But I need to fill this space fast…I'm starting to drool!
Now I'm feeling desperate and it's time to go
Down to the picture room—it's a lost cause, I know.
One last idea before the flash hits my eyes…
I may have a really cool built-in disguise.
I'm smiling now—it's ten o-eight…
One thing I discovered…my tongue worked great!

DRAGON'S COLD

If you ever meet a dragon with a cold,
There are some things you ought to know.
You should always stay clear of a dragon when it sneezes,
Or else you will be covered in a snotty lava flow.
It's oozy and icky and burning hot—
And will have a greenish-red hue.
So it would be in your very best interest
Not to let the dragon sneeze all over you!
One more piece of advice before I forget…
When a dragon coughs you'll quickly want to duck,
Because fire will shoot out of its' mouth…
And if you're in the way—you'll be out of luck!
So take it from me—a dragon doctor…
These creatures are very cranky when they're feeling bad.
And I'm thankful I only have missing eyebrows,
Because there are worse dragon patients I could have had!

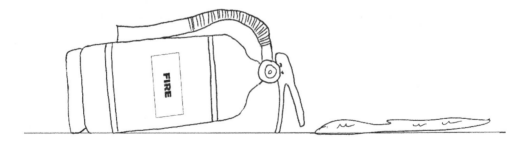

BETTY ATE SPAGHETTI

Betty ate spaghetti—that's all she ever ate.
Every morning, noon and night she had it on her plate.
Spaghetti pancakes and spaghetti sandwiches too!
Spaghetti casseroles and even spaghetti stew.
She twirled it on a fork and sucked the noodles up.
Once she even blended it and drank it from a cup!
Her parents tried to warn her and her teachers did too,
That eating the same thing all the time is not smart to do.
Betty kept eating spaghetti—and one day she said,
"I think the color of my hair is turning a little red".

That should have made her think twice—but it didn't stop her still…
She kept eating and eating and eating spaghetti UNTIL…
A noodle sprouted from her head—then another and another.
Betty looked in the mirror in horror and screamed for her mother.
Her mother took her to the doctor—he didn't know what to say.
He'd never seen anything like it before, and scratched his head in dismay!
Betty had spaghetti hair, and she began smelling like it too.
And it grew so fast and long, she didn't know what to do?
Her mother started cutting it when it grew down to her feet…
And now Betty finally knew why people say, "You are what you eat!"

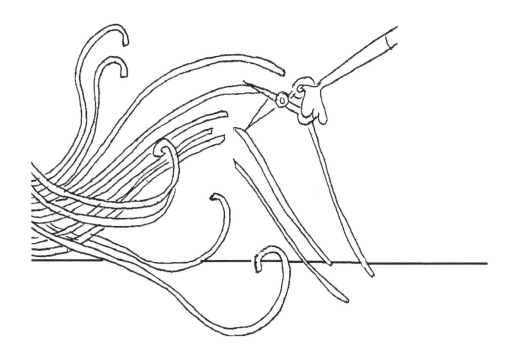

LAND OF UPSIDE DOWN

There's a place called the Land of Upside Down,
And when you first arrive it looks like everyone has a frown.
Until you walk like they do on the ceiling instead of the ground.
Here the coolest spikiest hairstyles can be found.
You'll notice their upside down bats sleep standing up,
And you hold your glass the opposite way to fill up your cup.

You have to remember to tuck your shirt in—so it's not in your face,
And girls have to wear magnetic skirts to keep them in place.
They eat a lot of upside down cake—which isn't bad at all,
And the upside down pizza casserole was pretty good, as I recall.
I'd recommend visiting the Land of Upside Down, as I once did years ago.
Just remember which way is which, because it's really hard to know!

LEMONADE

Lemonade for sale!
Lemonade for sale!
It's only twenty-five cents a cup.
Lemonade for sale!
Lemonade for sale!
Why don't you stop and fill up?
Look, I have my first customer!
How many cups would you like?
I'm saving up to buy myself a cool bike!
You say you only have a five-dollar bill?
Would you like a refill?
I don't have any money yet in my sack.
Unless you don't want any change back?

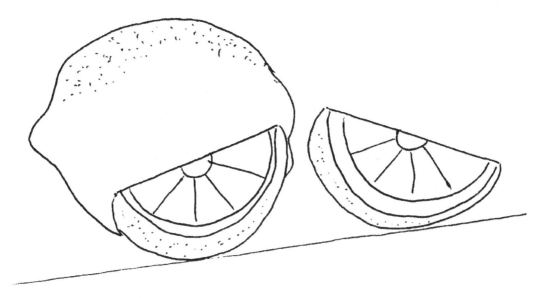

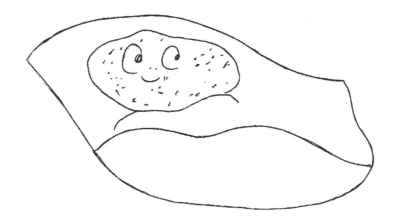

PET ROCK

I like my pet rock and he likes me.
I gave him some eyes so he can see.
He doesn't need food or water at all,
And he can fit in my pocket because he's so small.
I can carry him around anywhere,
And I don't have to brush him because he has no hair.
He doesn't bark or scratch or bite—
And he sleeps on my pillow every night!

DAVEY SPROCKET'S ROCKET

You say you haven't heard the story about little Davey Sprocket?
He wanted to visit space but he didn't have a rocket.
It's true Davey didn't have a rocket…but that didn't bother him though.
He thought, and thought, and thought until one day he said, "I know!"

"I'll drink all the soda and eat all the chili in this place,
Until I get really gassy…then I will toot, toot, toot right into space!"
"That's what I'll do…it sounds like a really good plan!"
Davey grabbed a can of chili, and so his mission began!

He ate about a 100 cans of chili…all that he found,
And he drank all the gassiest sodas around.
Until all of a sudden it was a huge surprise,
Out came the biggest toot—and Davey couldn't believe his eyes!

Up, up, up he went faster than a rocket!
Toot, toot, toot…went Davey Sprocket!
He shot into the atmosphere and out into the stars.
Then he tooted a few times more and went past mars!

Davey zoomed across the black hole, and back around the moon,
And he tried to do another toot…but it didn't come as soon.
"Oh, no", he said "I don't have any more chili to fuel my body rocket,"
Down, down, down fell Davey Sprocket!

He headed back down to earth—it was quite a sight to see!
And it was a miracle he fell right back to the place he wanted to be.
In a big pile of leaves in his backyard Davey did fall,
But when he opened his eyes he wondered if he'd gone anywhere at all?

Suddenly Davey heard his mom ask, "Where have you been?"
"You wouldn't believe it if I told you," he said with a grin.
"I hope you're hungry we're having your favorite chili for dinner tonight."
That was nice but Davey thought—he couldn't eat one more bite!

NUMB

It's been an hour of dental care,
And I'm still stuck in this sweaty dental chair!
It doesn't seem to hurt at all,
But I am so bored of staring at the wall!
My lip is sliding down my face,
But I can't even feel a trace!
And I'm sure I don't look very cool,
Talking with a big mouthful of drool!
The dentist keeps cramping my style,
By making me laugh with a lop-sided smile!
I sure feel silly and dumb,
When my mouth is really numb!

MY ROBOT IS SO STUBBORN!

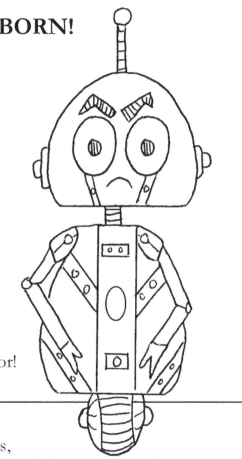

My robot is so stubborn!
He's as difficult as can be!
I built him to do my chores,
But now he's ignoring me!

He won't pick up my laundry,
And he won't make my bed!
He won't clean the kitty box,
He'll just frown and turn his head!

He won't take the garbage out,
And he won't vacuum the floor!
He won't do any dusting at all,
He shakes his head and slams the door!

My robot is so ungrateful,
I built him from head to wheel.
But when I complained to my parents,
They just said, "Now you know how we feel!"

WORLD'S STRONGEST SPIDER

Have you met Sid, the world's strongest spider, yet?
I met him the other day and it's something I regret!
I didn't believe all the stories I'd heard.
I thought they sounded really absurd…
Big muscles on an arachnid—no way!
Impossible—that's what you say.
I stumbled upon Sid down at the dock.
I'd just got some fish and chips, and saw him near a rock.
He said something to me…he wanted my food.
I wasn't about to give it up…I was in a pretty bad mood!
He showed me his big muscles and his tiny tattoos,
And told me I shouldn't cross him, because I'd surely lose.

"Give me your cod!" Sid yelled at me.
I said, "No," and then he grabbed me by my knee.
He said, "Listen dude! I'm warning you one last time,
Give up your cod or you are mine!"
I should have prepared for what was to come,
But I still thought fighting with a spider was dumb.
Then all at once he whirled me around,
Spun his strong web and he had me bound.
He picked me up and slammed me down,
And now my run-in with Sid is the talk of the town.
So please only go to the dock if you dare,
And if you do…at least buy some extra cod to share!

SUE LYNN

Sue Lynn loved wearing her tutu!
She wore it wherever she was at!
Even when she went poo-poo…
It was on her while she sat!
People thought she was cuckoo…
For doing that!

YELLOW SNOW

Snow is falling and school is out!
This is what I'm talking about!
Throwing snow balls and building snowmen—
I can't believe it's snowing again!
Making snow cones from the snow on the ground.
Look, here comes my Bassett Hound!
Umm…it doesn't look like he's playing.
I wouldn't eat that yellow snow—I'm just saying!

BAGPIPER

"The bagpiper is down!"
"The bagpiper is down!"
The news has spread fast
All through our Scottish town.
The bagpiper was piping,
And tripped on a stone.
He fell on his face…
Does anyone have a phone?
"The bagpiper is down!"
"The bagpiper is down!"
No more sight of his kilt,
In the colors of plaid and brown.
The bagpiper is okay,
But won't be piping for a bit.
His noggin they say,
Has taken quite a hit!
"The bagpiper is down!"
"The bagpiper is down!"
No music day and night,
Since he hit his crown!
Now it's really quiet,
You can't even hear a peep.
So everyone is trying to hurry,
And catch up on their sleep!

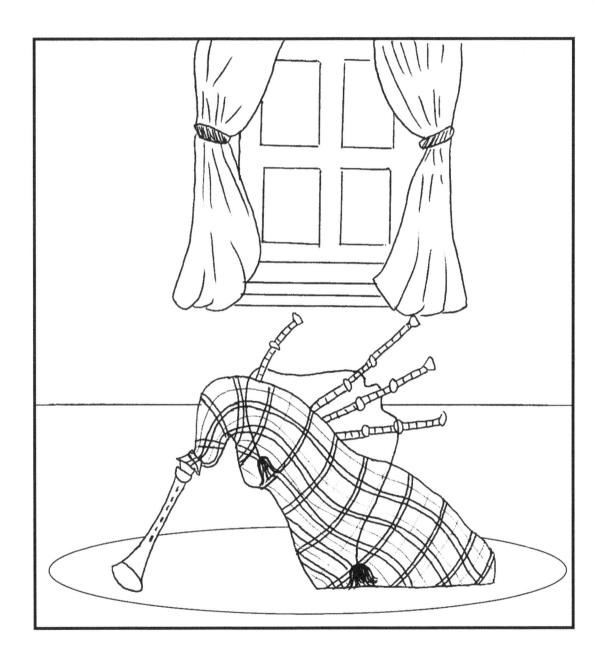

CRAYON

A dog named Crayon left a mark wherever he went,
And he needed a lot of cleanup because he always left a paw print.
He ran in circles, and a circle appeared…which was really strange—
And depending on his mood the color of his paw prints would change.
When Crayon was sad his paw prints would be blue,
And in a minute, when his mood changed, another color he drew.
Red paw prints meant he was mad and wanted to be left alone,
And green signaled he was hungry and he needed a bone!
Yellow paw prints were a sign he was happy and wanted to play,
And nobody knew what he was thinking when his paw prints turned grey.
Sometimes you would see him stop and kind of squat down,
So I bet you know why the color you didn't want to see…was brown.

LOVE BUG

Beware of the love bug—
For he can strike without warning!
You can be fine one day,
And be googly-eyed the next morning.
It happens all the time—
In every country, city and state.
One minute you want to be left alone,
And the next minute you're on a date!
You know you've been bitten
When your heart starts beating fast.
You walk around in a daze,
And you have a permanent smile like a cast!
There's no stopping the love bug,
Because he always gets his way.
He can make you act silly anytime…
But be especially careful on Valentine's Day!

O

Round and round a circle will go
Where it ends I do not know?
Sometimes it acts as the letter "O"
Unless it's busy being zero!

TINY PUMPKIN

Most people like big pumpkins,
But I like them small.
In fact—yesterday at the pumpkin patch,
I got the smallest pumpkin of all!
It was difficult to carve—
I had to use a magnifying glass to see.
You can't really tell it from the picture…
But that's my tiny pumpkin and me!

FRECKLES

Fran looked in the mirror
And saw even more freckles than before.
Five more must have appeared overnight…
Now she counted about ninety-four!
Some freckles were really big,
But most were so small she could barely see.
They looked like the stars in the sky,
Her face reminded her of the galaxy!
This gave Fran a great idea!
So she took a pen from the drawer—
To outline the big dipper,
Looking closer she saw even more!

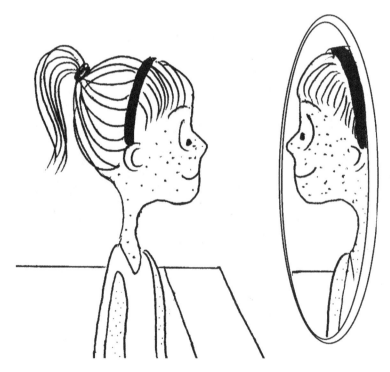

The little dipper was so cute—
She had to connect the dots on that too!
Next she saw Orion, the Great Hunter,
And the lion, the swan, the bears—who knew?
The constellations appeared on Fran's face,
Faster than you can say, "Milky Way!"
Her face began to look like a star map,
And this was sure to be the end to a perfect day!
But then Fran heard her dad's voice
Asking her where she had been.
He was down the hall working on a special project…
And couldn't find his very permanent marker pen!

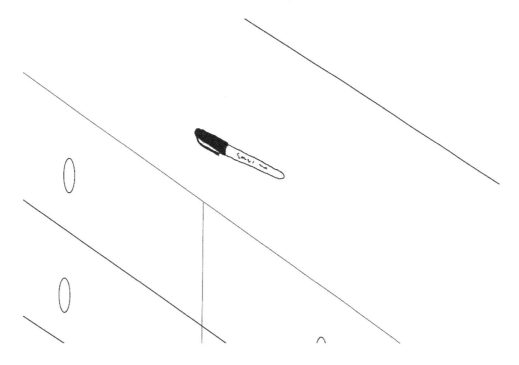

A GORILLA PLAYED ON MY SWING SET

A gorilla played on my swing set,
I just saw him the other day.
A gorilla played on my swing set,
And it looked like he wanted to stay!
He swung on the monkey bars,
And slid down the slide.
He went up and down the poles,
And jumped from side-to-side!
He was having so much fun,
I didn't want to bother him at all.
It was cool to see a gorilla play—
He had to be about 6 feet tall!

He must have escaped from the zoo?
That's all I can think of now.
Maybe he wanted a vacation,
And picked my backyard somehow?
But when I went to get my camera phone,
I came back and he was gone.
There was no sign of him anywhere,
Except for some footprints on the lawn!
I am so bummed that I missed him,
And I still can't believe what I have seen.
I say, "What's this gorilla mask doing on the floor?"
My sister says, "It's dad's costume for Halloween!"

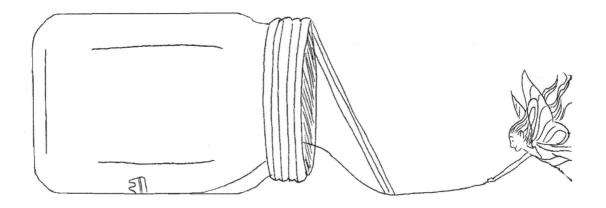

TOOTH FAIRY TRAP

Every time I lose a tooth I get another chance,
To set the tooth fairy trap again and be the first to get a glance.
I've made a special trap with a jar and some strings,
And I stay awake at night until I hear the flutter of her wings.
Tip-toe, tip-toe, that's what she usually does.
I try to pull the trap about then but she's never where she was!
She's a tricky little fairy—I've never seen her yet,
But I still have a lot of teeth to lose…and one night I'll catch her, I bet!

GAMER'S DIARY

Today I played on my personal handheld device until about noon.
Then I went to the store and bought a cool game called *Snake Dune*.
After that…I downloaded a game I found on the internet,
And played against my friends—I almost couldn't find my headset!
My mom brought my dinner into my room, and I ate between levels.
But it's hard to eat when you are fighting against snakes, soldiers, and devils!
Then my sister wanted to play with me—but I had no time,
I was on my headset figuring out how to defeat Master Slime!
I can report I got to the highest level, and finally beat the game.
I have the number one score—I even got to type in my name!
My parents just popped into my room and told me to go to bed.
They said, "No more video games, and your eyes look really red."
Until tomorrow my gamer friends—today was fun without a doubt!
You know whoever doesn't play video games is sure missing out!

MY SHADOW

My shadow does magic tricks,
I'm told by people I know.
Everyone is amazed by my shadow—
They applaud me wherever I go!
My shadow pulls rabbits out of hats,
And does coin tricks for Mr. McGroff.
One time it caused such a stir
When the rabbit's head fell off!
But then people discovered
It was a magic prop all along.
That only happens when a good trick
Goes terribly, terribly wrong!
But I haven't seen any of these tricks yet—
I've even tried looking in mirrors.
Because the best trick my shadow does…
Is the one when it disappears!

B.O.

Hello, I'm Bernie O'Shea…
And I haven't showered today.
Actually, I haven't showered for weeks!
My friends call me B.O.
Because they most certainly know,
To hold their noses—'cause my smell really reeks!

TRIPP THE DOUBLE DIPPER

They call me Tripp the Double Dipper,
I don't know why they do?
My dipping techniques are perfect,
I don't think they have a clue.
At parties I don't head to the games…
I go straight for the food.
Ranch dip is my dipping favorite,
But they say how I dip is rather rude.
I slather my carrots with dressing,
Then scrape the extra into the bowl.
Too much dressing is really fattening,
And too many snacks can take a toll!
When it comes to cheese dip,
The chip has to be covered not leaving a spot.
Sometimes I have to dip once more,
After I take a bite and realize it's not.
But lately at parties it's been different,
People rush to the snack table really fast.
By the time I get to the dip it's gone—
Now I'm the one who's dipping last.

SUNSCREEN

Suzie's mom told her to use sunscreen.
I guess she should have known,
That if she didn't apply it carefully,
It would surely make her groan.
For after all the swimming fun,
And the hours in the sun she spent,
Her skin was a painful lobster red—
Except for the spot with the white hand print!

A TOUR OF THE SCHOOL CAFETERIA

In the school cafeteria you'll hear the sound of whimpered cries,
As the lunch ladies pile our plates with green wiener wraps and greasy fries!
On some days it looks like the food is piled on our trays about 10 feet high!
With things like rubbery toasted cheese sandwiches and pizza pie!

Then the bargaining begins with the kids that brought their lunch.
We say things like, "This hamburger sure has a delicious crunch."
Or, "I'll give you whatever this is if you give me your PB & J."
And if you're lucky the kid will take pity and say, "Okay."

But then there are days like today when luck is not on your side.
So you take a drink of the old milk and swallow your pride.
Your stomach is growling, and you try not to think as you take a bite.
Then you eat the pile of unnamed casserole with all of your might!

Yes, the school cafeteria is an interesting place, it's true!
And maybe they're designed to build a kid's character too?
You'll always smell the recognizable stench in the air.
I suppose the cafeteria isn't too bad—if you like to eat food on a dare!

CONTEST

Marcus did a deep-pitched one,
And Mike's went on forever!
John's was intermittent—
They were all pretty clever!
I was selected to be the judge.
It was hard to choose the best.
My friends all did a great job…
In our lunchtime belching contest!

BOOK WORM

I couldn't wait until library class
To show him his new home!
He squirmed in my pocket,
And he wrapped around my comb.
But the library teacher didn't love him
The way I thought she would.
She screamed at the top of her lungs,
And said I was up to no good!
You see, the quiet library went into a panic—
Soon it looked like it had been in a blast.
Papers were flying as I tried to catch him,
But he moved surprisingly fast!
He wiggled into the fiction section,
And I never would have bet,
That all that chaos could have happened,
Just from giving the librarian a book worm pet!

LULA AND HER HULA HOOP

What does Lula have?
A hula hoop!
What is she doing?
Twirling it in a loop!
What just happened?
It started to droop!

ROCA

Lately I don't have to clean the litter,
And my dog no longer eats my socks.
Now his treats come from the Roca
He finds in the kitty litter box!

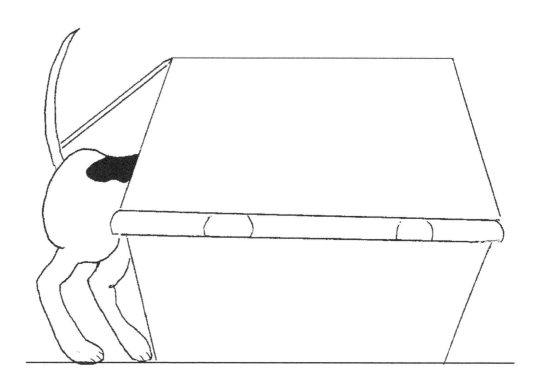

THE PORCUPINE AND RACCOON

Poor little porcupine had no friends.

No one wanted to be around him because of his sharp ends.

So he decided since he was already close to the ground,

He'd pass the time by picking up all the trash he found.

Before long a huge pile of garbage was stuck to his back—

Wads of paper towels, leftover food, and even a plastic sack!

There was so much trash that he could barely see,

And then he thought, "Who's going to get this off of me?"

Porcupine worried as he waddled down the road,

How would he ever get rid of his heavy load?

Just then he stumbled upon a raccoon looking for something to eat.

The raccoon couldn't believe he was seeing a moving pile of trash with feet!

"Hello there," said the porcupine to the raccoon, "How do you do?"

And the raccoon looked at the pile of talking trash and said, "What are you?"

"I'm a porcupine—I know you can't tell,"

But would you be willing to help me out? I'm not doing so well."

The raccoon felt sorry for the porcupine who was trying to do a good deed,

And he didn't want to say, "No" to his new friend in need.

So with his fingers he began carefully removing the garbage one–by–one.
He found some tasty treats and thought helping the porcupine was fun!
The raccoon found the leftover food made a really nice meal,
And the porcupine learned how happy having a friend made him feel.
Then the porcupine said, "I'm not sure what I'll do when you're gone?"
The raccoon replied, "Don't worry friend—I've got your back from now on."

MONSTER IN THE CLOSET

You say there's a monster in your closet?
I'd be glad to take a look.
I'll just open up this door…
Oh—I found a book!
And a half eaten chicken leg
Under a big pile of toys.
If there is something in here,
Then how come I don't hear any noise?
Why are you telling me to wait?
Ouch! I think I just found your monster bait!

MY DOG FLOSSED HIS TEETH

My dog flossed his teeth!
I saw him just the other night.
He carefully wrapped the floss
Around his toe nails really tight!
He started with his front incisors,
And got a lot of plaque out in between.
Then he flossed around his canine teeth,
Until his gums were really clean!
His molar teeth had bits of biscuits
Stuck in them way in the back.
Not to mention the trace of noodles
From when I shared my leftover mac.
It's cool my dog can floss his teeth,
And he's just a little over four.
But I wish he'd learn another good habit...
Not to go potty on our floor!

ATHLETE'S FOOT

Malcolm the quarterback had really smelly feet!
He hadn't changed his socks for a year!
And the fact is the smell was so hideously bad,
You didn't have to see him to know that he was near!
Malcolm didn't care, and he refused to change his socks,
Because he thought they brought him good luck.
But the only thing they seemed to bring him at first,
Were flies and a lingering smell like a garbage truck!
But one day something started sprouting from his socks,
And finally they ripped apart at the seams.
The sprout grew so fast and the stench was so bad,
It was something you would only see in bad dreams!
Tiny buds in the shape of helmets started to appear,
And the smell was much worse than before.

Pretty soon the helmets grew so fast and large
That Malcolm couldn't even walk anymore!
That's when the coach told everyone not to panic,
And he put a clothes pin on his nose.
Then stooped down to take a closer look,
And said, "I think it's a bad case of athlete's foot, I suppose."
Then one-by-one the helmets started falling off,
Just like fruit would from a rancid vine.
And to everyone's surprise, they didn't smell at all—
The helmets even had a really cool design.
It turned out the socks really did bring Malcolm good luck,
Because his team mates got helmets for free.
Now Malcolm is wearing a brand new pair of lucky socks.
Maybe they'll get matching uniforms next year—we'll see?

ANIMAL CRACKERS

Animal crackers are my favorite.
They march across the table.
It's always a dangerous journey,
Because of my hungry dog Mabel.
The hippos swim in my milk,
And the monkeys do flips off my cup.
The seals like to float on top,
Until I decide to eat them up.
The elephant's trunks are tasty,
And the camel's humps are divine.
Sometimes they all line up
Neatly in a single file line.
Then it's time to meet their fate…
Each one first loses its tail.
And the only way an animal escapes,
Is if it happens to be a little stale!

GROWING PAINS

They say they're growing pains,
But I don't really know?
I have a pain in my eye,
And a cramp in my toe!
My elbow is killing me,
And my knees hurt bad!
My fingers are tender,
And my heels hurt like mad!
I sense my muscles stretching!
My bones feel like rubber bands!
There is irritation in my shoulder,
And I have cramps in my hands!
I tell you my body is a mess!
There are twinges in my spine!
It's funny with all these growing pains…
My brain feels fine?

CONNECTED

You might say I'm connected—
Literally, I think you'll see!
I've got piercings and hoops
On every square inch of me!
People stop to check me out
And are in utter shock and horror!
When I tell them I'm not done,
And I'm planning to get some more.
My lips are looped together,
So I must eat through a straw.
And I have more chains on me
Than a bicycle or an electric saw!
I never go too close to magnets,
With all this metal you see.
And metal detectors are the worst,
Not to mention airport security!
Now that my piercings are connected,
With these chains I can barely walk.
But I think I look freakishly cool,
Too bad I can barely talk!
Expressing myself feels really good—
These chains make me feel so free.
The only problem is I used a lock…
And accidentally lost the key!

HAROLD

There is one fact about Harold
I bet you didn't know.
He's got three separate stomachs—
All his food knows where to go!
The smallest one is for vegetables,
And anything healthy and green.
His next biggest stomach is for fast food,
And other food on commercials he's seen.
His biggest stomach just keeps growing—
It's the one that holds all the dessert.
But now he has a bigger problem…
He can't fit all his stomachs in his shirt!

CROOKED HOUSE

Have you seen the crooked house
On the crooked hill?
Have you stepped inside it
And almost took a spill?
When you stood up straight
Did you lean against your will?
I bet you stumbled around
Until you got your fill?
Did you get really dizzy
And look as green as a dill?
Did you go to the store
And buy a motion sickness pill?
Will you visit the crooked house again
When you have some time to kill?
And if you do, I hope you've practiced...
The vomit recovery drill!

NAIL SNAILS

People have told me not to bite my nails,
But I never thought it was true!
They warned the germs would make me sick,
But if they only knew!
What I've discovered is most horrifying,
And even worse than the flu!
My grimy nails are hosts to nail snails,
And I never had a clue!
Down in the depths of my cuticles they lurk,
Oh so slimy and blue!
And really like the taste of my tongue,
With every nervous chew!
And as for my teeth they are not spared,
Because they eat right through!
So a warning to all you nail biters out there—
Keep biting…and you may get nail snails too!

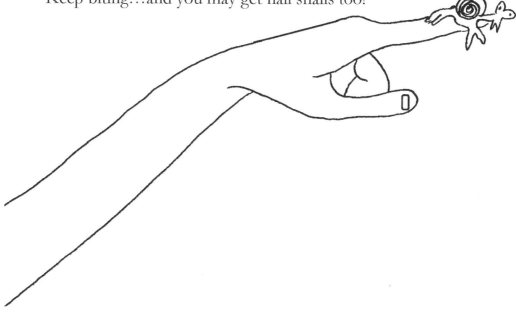

LOU

Hello I am Lou,
and I am one big tattoo—
Some think I look bizarre!
But I'm proud of my tats—
Look at these colorful rats!
On my arm there's this beautiful car.

Yes I am Lou,
And I advertise too—
I advertise near and far.
I enjoy where I work—
And this is my perk…
I get free tattoos every day from Star!

TATTOO

Hey this is Lou,
And the ink parlor crew—
The ink parlor crew we are!
Our mission is simple,
To cover your pimple,
With a pretty rose or a cool guitar.

Dude this is Lou—
Why are you feeling blue?
And blue you really are!
My work's not guaranteed,
But I did succeed,
In making you look like an avatar!

BIRTHDAY?

It's my birthday today?
Has it already been another year?
The presents are great,
And everyone is here!
The food is delicious—
The fries are even curly,
But there's one small problem…
We're celebrating it three months early!

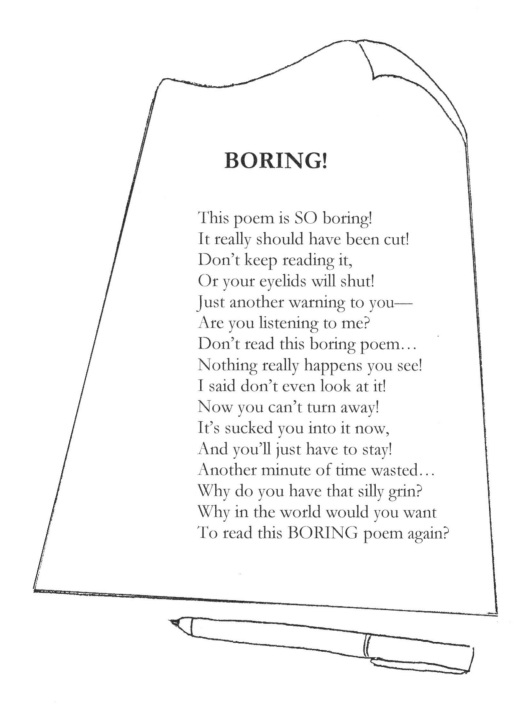

BORING!

This poem is SO boring!
It really should have been cut!
Don't keep reading it,
Or your eyelids will shut!
Just another warning to you—
Are you listening to me?
Don't read this boring poem…
Nothing really happens you see!
I said don't even look at it!
Now you can't turn away!
It's sucked you into it now,
And you'll just have to stay!
Another minute of time wasted…
Why do you have that silly grin?
Why in the world would you want
To read this BORING poem again?

BUNNY TRAIL

I thought the Easter bunny only left baskets,
But that isn't all he left for me last year.
I woke up on Easter morning excited,
And what I found I'm not sure you want to hear!
I now know what the bunny trail is,
And sadly it's not what people think!
A trail of chocolate colored pellets had appeared,
And I had to hold my nose 'cause it really did stink!

BIRDS

Look at those birds
Circling in the sky.
Right above my head,
Way up high.
Circling and circling,
I don't know why?
PLOP…they got me
On their first try!

HOLY MOLY

"Holy Moly!" is what my dad had said.
 I looked out the window as I got out of bed.
A bunch of mounds were in plain sight.
It appeared a holy moly had struck overnight!

I thought holy moly's were supposed to be good?
Attending church like a holy moly should!
Instead the holy moly caused us grief.
He needed to stop his bad behavior and turn a new leaf!

Our near perfect grass looked like piles of dirt…
And because of the holy moly we were on high alert!
I shouted to him, but he was nowhere to be seen.
That holy moly wasn't holy at all—he was mean!

But he didn't stay long—he went on his way.
No more mounds appeared every single day.
Now it looks like he's visiting our neighbors next door,
Because their yard now looks like ours did before.

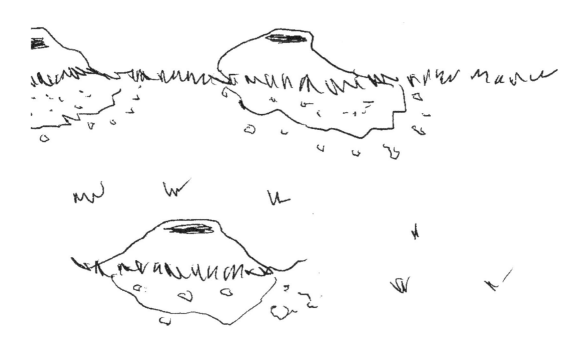

THANKSGIVING

I'm thankful for the dressing.
I'm thankful for the pie.
I'm thankful for the cranberries,
And that the turkey isn't dry!
I'm thankful for the sweet potatoes.
I'm thankful for the rolls.
I'm thankful for the olives,
So I can put my fingers in the holes!
I'm thankful for my grandma.
I'm thankful she didn't pinch my cheeks.
I'm thankful for my earplugs,
So I can't hear my baby cousin's squeaks!
I'm thankful for my patience.
I'm thankful my crazy family is here.
I'm thankful that Thanksgiving Day
Only comes around once a year!

SEAGULLS

At the beach I saw some seagulls, and I thought it was a blessing.
Until I saw them perched above the outdoor restaurant, and I was stressing!
For the woman who ordered a green salad with extra ranch dressing,
And who was distracted sitting underneath the seagull's who were messing!
But whether or not she took a bite—I'll have to leave you guessing.

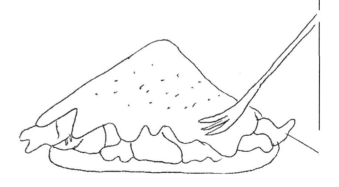

WATER FOUNTAIN

I'm not thirsty a bit—
My throat's just a little dry!
No, I'm not afraid to give
The water fountain another try!
I'm twisting the nozzle—
See it's working already!
A stream of water is flowing—
It's coming out steady.
I've got this mastered—
I'll turn it up a little more.
Oops, the water's too high—
Now there's water on the floor!
It's just really touchy…
The water is flowing low!

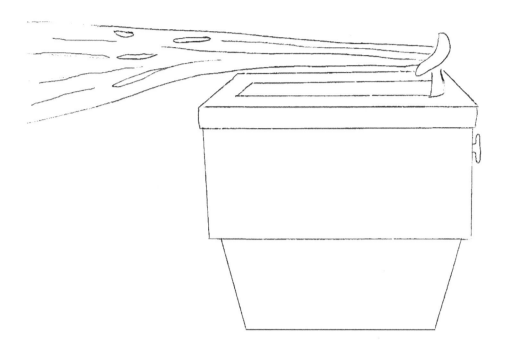

Now it's suddenly stopped—
What's happening? I don't know?
I'll check down beneath,
And bend down to take a peek,
To see if there's something stuck,
Maybe there's some kind of leak?
Nothing is coming out—
Dehydration is setting in,
And sadly I forgot to bring
My water bottle again!
This fountain is not my friend!
WHOA—water just squirted in my eye!
That's code for the water fountain saying…
Adios, sayonara, farewell and goodbye!

SECRET THUMB SUCKER'S CLUB

Not just anyone can join our secret Thumb Sucker's Club.
You have to have a special blanket with a favorite corner you rub.
The corner should be really dirty where it won't come out if you scrub.
And your thumb must look like you've spent hours soaking it in a tub.
Those are just a few requirements to be in our Secret Thumb Suckers Club!

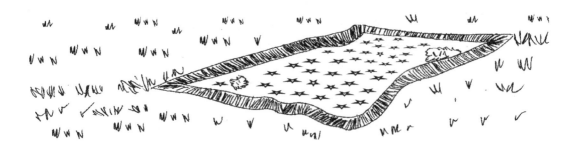

HORSERADISH SANDWICH

Oh give me a horseradish sandwich!
I'd like a quarter horse on wheat bread please—
And add an organic radish.
Actually, make that a palomino—
Quarter horses make me sneeze!

T.P.

I felt something strange on my shoe.
I thought it was doggy doo.
But I didn't have a clue—
Until a passerby was inclined,
To show me what I couldn't find,
And was way too kind,
To remove the trail of T.P.—
That was following me from behind!

GRANNY MAE'S GIANT CANDY CANE

Granny Mae used a giant candy cane.
It helped her walk for a little while.
Who knew she had such a sweet tooth?
Soon she was walking lopsided down the aisle!
Now her candy cane has disappeared,
But she sure has a really big smile!

LONG, LONG BEARD

It's terribly frightening
My long, long beard!
"You better not trim me,"
One day it sneered!
Those were the words
That I most feared!
When it saw the scissors
It spoke—and that's weird!
It just kept growing…
My long, long beard!
And I've tried to get help
But it always interfered!
So it seems I'm stuck
Inside my long, long beard!
Now I'm saying, "Bye,"
Because I've disappeared!

SPELLING BEE

Speling alwayz confuzes mee,
So I want to cach a speling bee!
I wil no wen to uz a K or a C,
And wen to uz an I befor E!
I'm serching dering resess franticlee,
Sens we hav a speling test at 3!

I'M NOT TICKLISH!

Tickling me is a waste of time,
So I wouldn't even try.
I'm not ticklish anywhere,
And I don't know the reason why?
No, I'm not ticklish one bit…
So I'd suggest not tickling my toes.
Don't try to tickle me under my chin,
And definitely not on my nose!
I'm not ticklish on my funny bone either,
Or even on my knee (hee, hee)
So try and try as you might—
You won't be able to tickle me!
I wouldn't tickle me on the back of my neck,
And especially not on my side.
By now you've probably figured out—
When I said I wasn't ticklish…I lied!

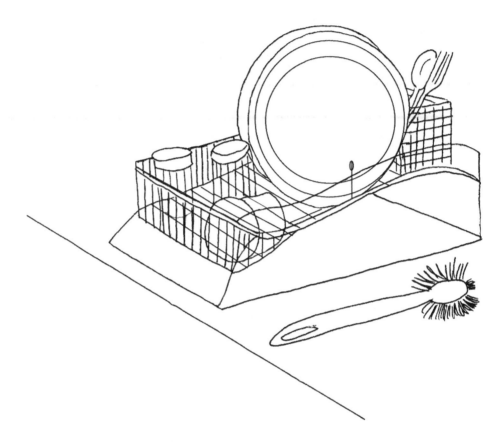

DIRTY DISHES

Jake found something in the closet that worked great
For scraping the grime that was stuck on the plate.
It helped him do his chore in a rush.
But after the dishes were done and dry,
His parents came to him and asked why,
He had chosen to use the toilet brush?

LAST SATURDAY'S GAME

My teammate passed me the basketball
During last Saturday's close game!
I dribbled as fast as I could down the court,
Since it was my fifteen seconds of fame!
I wove through the middle to get to the hoop,
And the fans started to motion and scream.
I jumped up and did a perfect slam dunk…
Too bad it was for the other team!

I LOST MY MIND

I just lost my mind!
I don't know where it went?
I looked under the sink,
And I reached down in the vent!
Is it under a rock or hiding in a tree?
How did my mind escape from me?
I'm calling out to my mind—
I wonder if it's on a trip?
Maybe it's on a cruise?
Or on the Las Vegas strip?
Oh, where did my mind go?
And if I find it—will I even know?

CAMEL

Did you see what that camel just did?
He spit right in my eye!
I told him I liked his humps,
And he spit and I'm not sure why?
Then he smugly looked at me
And slowly walked away.
His attitude needs some adjusting,
I think my mom would say.

MASON MCCREET

"I'm not hungry," said Mason McCreet.
"My stomach is full and I just can't eat.
I cannot take one more bite of this cold meat.
And you don't want to see what will happen if I eat this beet!
Why did that cookie just fall down from under my seat?
I was saving it for my after dinner treat!"

CAT

I watched as my cat ran
And did a wild skip,
Slid down the stairs
And rolled into a double flip!
Climbed up the curtains,
I wish he'd just get a grip!
But I guess I'm the one
Who gave him the catnip.

BEWARE!

The mountain is on high alert!
The flagged area is prepared!
The ski facility has people ready
In case something needs repaired!
The chairlift operators are on guard!
The rescue unit has been made aware!
My sister is putting on her skis again…
So everyone take cover and BEWARE!

ELEMENT OF SURPRISE

In last Friday's science class
Liz felt a sudden urge to pass,
While we were learning about the periodic table,
When out of her came the smelliest gas!
It sounded like a roar of thunder,
And everyone looked at her in wonder.
Then I raised my hand to ask,
"Which element of the table does that fall under?"

OUR TEACHER HAS THE WORST BREATH!

Our teacher has the worst breath!
It smells like a garbage dump!
I was thinking that's probably why
He is always such a grump.
When we're stumped on a question
We raise our hands and face the wrath,
Of a smell like rotten garlic bread
When we're trying to do our math!
After lunch is always the worst…
We hold our breath from smelling

His half-digested salami sandwich,
So we can't focus on our spelling!
We think he eats a can of sardines
Right before our reading class.
When he helps us with our words,
His breath smells like toxic gas!
We thought we'd get some relief
From the stench of moldy mouth fruit...
When our teacher called in sick one day,
But instead we got a gassy substitute!

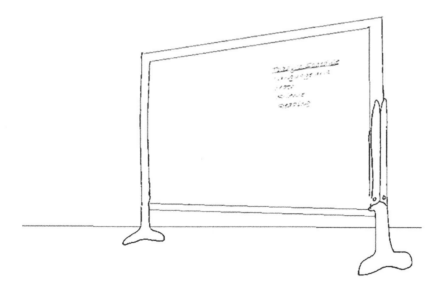

DOG PILE

I saw a dog pile a mile high!
It was really loud I tell you!
With a million different barks
From labs to poodles—it's true!

And they were all friendly—
Not one seemed to be mean.
But in time I did notice…
The dog pile began to lean!

All their wagging and panting
Caused them to fall like bricks.
Then I don't know what happened…
But I woke up to a hundred million licks!

ELECTION

My goat is political!
My goat is into the vote!
My goat loves his candidate
And he's not afraid to promote!
He eats the signs of competitors,
And just came out with a projection,
That I'm going to win by a landslide…
I didn't even know I was in the election!

BEANS

I shouldn't have fed beans to my dog!
I should've listened to my mom 'cause she knows...
How it feels to get out of bed in the morning,
And have recycled beans squish through her toes!

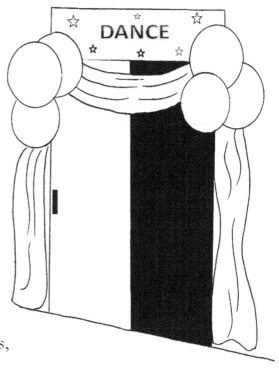

COOTIES

We never thought we'd see it!
I wonder if he's doing it on a dare?
Raymond is slow dancing with a girl—
She must have caught him unaware!
School dances are always scary.
They're riddled with danger and fear!
Girls are okay if they stay in their circles,
But once in a while they'll come near!
Doesn't Raymond know the secret?
Girls are known to have cooties galore!
I'm not sure what cooties actually do—
But it's something you shouldn't ignore!
Maybe he already has the cooties?
That's probably why he's acting like this!
Now she has her head on his shoulder!
Gross…I only hope they don't kiss!
My friends and I are watching this scene,
And are trying our best to be courageous!
Why did we agree to dance with those girls?
I think the cooties may be really contagious!

SWAMP SWIM

"Diaper baby!" is what my friend yells.
We are in the city pool and it really smells!
We just saw something unsightly float by—
The baby's diaper was off and he started to cry!
Spit and drool are in the water, which are always there.
And the whiff of chlorine and barf is in the air.
But this night happens to be the worst night of all...
Tonight the pool sort of turns into a bathroom stall!
It's our Halloween tradition to go to the Swamp Swim.
And I must say the water this evening looks pretty grim.
So if you want to do the scariest thing on Halloween night...
Go to the Swamp Swim at the pool—it's a frightening sight!

GLASSES

It's fuzzy, it's blurry—
I think I'm going blind!
My glasses aren't working,
Everything looks intertwined!
Maybe I have glaucoma?
There's a halo to my right…
And my pupils may be dilated—
Everything looks really bright!
My corneas are disrupted!
I know this can't be good!
I've sat too close to the T.V.
All through my childhood!
Now I guess I'm paying the price,
But I don't know braille one bit.
And I think my head is shrinking,
Because my glasses don't fit!
In fact they have fallen off…
Now I feel as blind as a bat.
Then I hear my mom yell,
"Where are my glasses at?"

INVISIBLE CHAMELEON

My invisible chameleon
Is a very special pet!
He's the best at camouflage,
Because I haven't seen him yet!
He doesn't change colors…
Of chameleon's he's most rare,
And has an unusual talent—
Of blending in with air!

CAMP DONTWANNAGO

The cabin smelled like a toilet!
And ants crawled all over my bed!
My friend on the bunk above me
Had drooled all over my head!

The name badges we had to make
Out of thin pieces of smelly wood,
All got ruined in the pouring rain,
And I brought a coat with no hood!

Swimming was supposed to be fun,
But there was algae everywhere!
Our towels were nowhere to be found,
And we left the water with green hair!

The bows and arrows were broken.
The food tasted like uncooked dough.
The songs we sang were way too lame,
And during the race I stubbed my toe!

Outdoor school has taught us one thing,
And something the teachers already know…
That we'd be begging to go back to school
By the end of our trip to Camp Dontwannago!

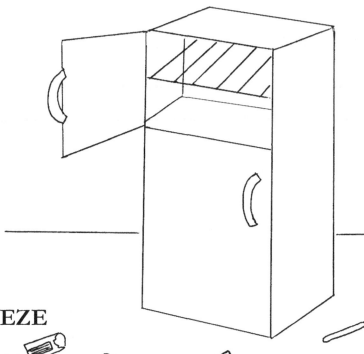

BRAIN - FREEZE

The pain is unbearable!
I think my brain has turned to ice!
I shouldn't have eaten the popsicles—
I went back to the freezer twice!
Then I ate ice cream cones,
And washed them down with a shake.
Enjoyed an ice cream sandwich—
I should have stopped for my sake.
I just finished the shaved ice snack,
And have fallen to my knees!
My head feels like an arctic weather zone—
Experiencing a massive brain-freeze!

GIGANTIC FERRIS WHEEL

Look at me I'm riding on the most gigantic Ferris wheel!
And I hope no screws are missing in these pieces of steel!
It's really high up here and I'm definitely beginning to feel
Like I should have not eaten that super-sized meal!
My stomach is turning from the smell of that kid's orange peel,
And from this height it feels like I might actually hurl for real!
I'm giving everyone down below a warning—this is not ideal,
That if they don't scatter like ants they are in for quite an ordeal!
So I'm hoping all of you down below heed my desperate appeal,
Or you might see a lot more of me than I wanted to reveal!
The operator has now stopped the ride—he knows the deal!
Oh no…it's too late—I just christened someone's automobile!

PUCKER FACE

Brianna thought it was her place
To give her baby sister Grace
Her first taste of a lemon—
And watch her pucker face!

SNACKS

Can you guess my favorite snack?
They're tasty to eat!
And are pure protein—
Better than a plate of meat!
Chocolate covered ants
Are certainly delicious,
And wiggly squiggly worms
Are surprisingly nutritious!
When fried they provide
Just the right crunch,
And make great appetizers
Right before lunch.
Bacon flavored crickets
Are perfect with scrambled eggs.
Just remember to floss your teeth—
'Cause they'll be filled with little legs!

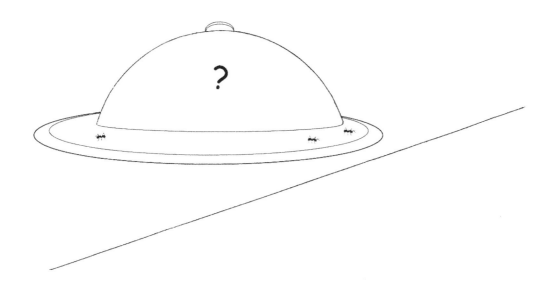

DON'T YOU KNOW?

We're all the same under our skin—
Red, black, brown, yellow, white,
Women, babies, children, and men!
So treat each other kindly since this is true...
We all bleed the same red blood—
Except for the space alien making faces at you!

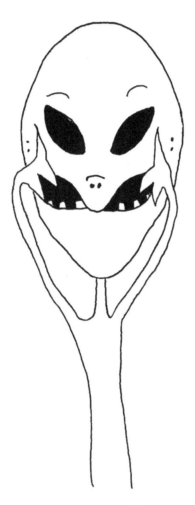

MAGIC SOMBRERO

"Try this magic sombrero on," the salesman said.
I was a little hesitant, but it was a cool shade of red.
So I picked it up gently, and it spun in the air…
And I knew then this sombrero, was indeed very rare!
For it rested upon my head, and Spanish music played.
The sound of maracas and guitars, this sombrero made!
But I'm afraid there is more, and the worst is yet to come…
The hat started pounding my head like a drum!
And I couldn't take it off, because it was stuck to my head!
It felt like it was sucking my brain, and I knew I'd been misled!
The salesperson acted like he had seen this all before.
He didn't try to help, and he just stared at the floor!
I couldn't hear what he said, so he held up a sign—
It read: "If you buy this sombrero you'll be just fine!"
I dug for money, because I didn't want to take out a loan
For a torturous magic sombrero, I didn't want to own!
But the pounding was so loud, and the suction made me weak,
I bought the sombrero under a questionable sales technique!
Now I have the magic sombrero, and I don't know what to do?
Hey—this sombrero would really look great on you!

AUGUSTUS

Augustus is pose'n
In his new lederhosen
That he has just chosen
But suddenly stands frozen
When he realizes something needs close'n!

LOST

I admit I'm directionally challenged.
I don't know where I am one bit!
I've tried every path to get out!
Now I'm lost and here I sit!
I'm calling out to be rescued,
And hopefully it won't take them days.
I've seen a lot of skeletons around…
Probably more victims of this corn maze!

CAT FEVER

My cat gave me cat fever…
I know it's true!
He has the sniffles,
And maybe even the flu!
He coughed and hacked,
And barfed up some fur.
He sneezed on my face—
It's all such a blur!
I heard cat fever
Is going around?
And his faint meow
Has a raspy sound!
So you don't believe me?
My forehead is burning!
Before I lose my voice—
I'm in no shape for learning!

I have to stay home!
Why are you shaking your head?
You say I don't have a fever?
Please…I need to go back to bed!
So hear my desperate plea—
I got this virus from cat drool,
And I have the cat fever,
So I can't go to school!
Now you're looking for our cat,
And ask me, "Where did he go?"
Oh no, you found him purring
And sitting by the window.
Well that blew my cover—
I shouldn't of used my pet.
This story worked great for my friend,
But I guess his dad isn't a vet!

HAIRCUT

I don't know how it happened?
This haircut is not what I planned!
I wanted to find a new cool style,
Because my hair was looking bland.
Now it's sticking up in places
I never even knew existed.
And what's left of my bangs,
Now seem distorted and twisted.
There is even a few bald spots—
It's a good thing the cut was free.
I'd blame it on the barber,
But this haircut was from me!

PANIC

My dog's tongue had gone crazy!
It was not under his control!
Faster and faster it went
With every twist and roll.
He had a look about him…
He was in a state of panic!
His eyes were like golf balls—
They looked gigantic!
And I was really worried
That his health was going south!
Until I saw the peanut butter…
Stuck to the roof of his mouth!

CARL THE KICKBOXING KANGAROO

On the open ranges of Australia
There is a tale of a creature so rare.
He's big and red and stands on two legs,
And makes people stop and stare!
By now you may have guessed it,
Or at least have a small clue...
The creature I'm referring to
Is Carl, the Kickboxing Kangaroo!
He could be the first Heavyweight Kangaroo.
His left hook is something to be seen.
He's set to be a champion in the arena—
A lean mean fighting machine!
He practices his craft on a punching bag
His owner had shipped for his use.
And contenders line up to fight him—
I guess they really like the abuse!
Carl's kick is what he's known for—
It's an impressive sight to behold.
The power in his legs is amazing,
And anyone that sees his skills is sold!
But there is a small problem Carl has had,
And could affect his kickboxing destiny…
He hasn't won a single kickboxing fight yet—
Because he keeps knocking out the referee!

FINGERLESS FRED

"Fingerless Fred how do you play a piano
Without any fingers?", you say.
"It's easy…you do it this way:
First, you have to be creative.
I sometimes use my toes,
And when their tired I use my nose!"
"Fingerless Fred that is very impressive,
I have to give credit to you,
Is that what you really do?"
"Yes, but if you ever see me laughing
And the music is a bit off tone,
You'll know I had to use my funny bone!"

FUNDRAISER

At school they are doing a fundraiser,
And selling pencils that smell.
All different smells they are offering,
"Come take a whiff!" they yell.
And they say, "There's a special today—
You buy five and get a mystery one free.
That's a great deal you can't pass up,
You'll love the smells—you'll see!
We have banana, bubblegum, root beer,
Cotton candy and even cupcake!
Gourmet flavors that you'll just love,
Like French fries and caramel shake!
The lemon-lime ones are going fast—
And it's time to pay up you know.
Hurry up because there's a long line,
So please choose your pencils and go!"
I went ahead and chose my five pencils,
And they threw in the mystery one too.
What a great deal that would have been…
If the mystery one didn't smell like poo!

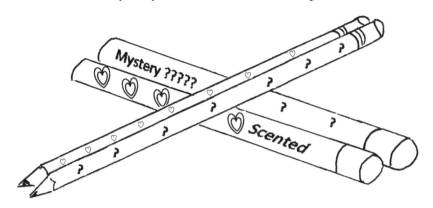

BANANA SPLIT

When you do a banana split,
Or even when you sit,
Be sure that your pants fit…
Or else you might find a slit,
In a place you don't want to get!

ELEVATOR

"Help, this is an emergency!
The elevator is stuck!"
It's packed like sardines—
This is just my luck!
I was headed on my way
To a very important place.
Now I am unfortunately in
Everyone's personal space!
I'm not claustrophobic,
But I'm squirming just a bit.
I was headed to the bathroom.
I'm trying hard to forget
How much I have to go!
I'm sure the smell will be a clue.
People are holding their breath,
Because it smells like poo!
I shouldn't of eaten eggs,
Or the broccoli last night.

The others are backing away—
I guess they have every right!
The elevator is now working.
The doors will soon be open.
I'm sure to smell fresh air
Is what everyone is hopin'!
The doors are opening up!
People are running out!
And the people coming in
Know I'm guilty without a doubt!
As I walk out of the elevator,
I see their faces look green.
They're giving me dirty looks—
Blaming me for this toxic scene!
So I guess I learned a lesson,
No matter what you do…
Don't step inside an elevator
If you have to go number two!

MY CAT PLAYS VIDEO GAMES

My cat sat by me watching
Every video game move I made!
I thought it was because he loved me,
But I would soon feel betrayed!
I discovered what the real truth was,
He wanted to learn the tricks,
Of shooting down the bad guys,
And doing those cool ninja kicks!
He always tries to play innocent,
But the other day after lunch,
I came back into my room to see,
A screenshot of a face punch!
He sat there purring at me,
And massaging the controller,

Then suddenly a grenade was thrown,
And it took out my main patroller!
With his head he nudged the trigger,
To launch missiles at my troops,
And since my guys were unprepared,
He took out all of my groups!
I'm worried these games are too violent,
And they are not intended for cats!
He needs to stop playing them at once,
And go back to chasing rats!
For his own good I must stop him,
I will have to show him the door!
And I'll need to do it really fast…
Before he beats my all-time highest score!

JERRY MCNAIRY

"I'll give you two bucks if you chew that old wad of gum stuck to the chair!"
This is the type of thing Jerry McNairy will do on a dare!
And how about eating that half-eaten sandwich in the garbage can?
If you can't find anyone else to eat it—just ask Jerry, he's your man!
He's built a reputation for taking on the grossest dares people dish out.
I can't remember any dare he didn't do—he's even licked a pig's snout!
But he doesn't provide this type of disgusting entertainment for free,
Daring Jerry always involves paying him some kind of fee!
People have spent their whole allowances watching Jerry do his dares.
It's crazy what he'll do for some money and a few laughs and stares!
Now after all of the dares he's done, he's gotten to be pretty wealthy…
But he's sick a lot and can't spend it—because he just ain't very healthy!

MY SISTER'S COOKING

My sister just started cooking—
I hope we will survive!
Last week she served us a casserole,
And instead of one teaspoon of pepper…
She had put in five!

We tried to eat a cake she cooked,
And she said it was my fault
For mixing up the order of ingredients,
And instead of using sugar…
She used salt!

Yesterday she made fruit and yogurt parfaits—
We hadn't eaten good in days!
We thought she couldn't mess it up,
But instead of using yogurt…
She used mayonnaise!

My parents are trying to be polite—
Telling her she's a much better cook.
Saying that practice makes perfect,
And are now busy trying to hide…
The recipe book!

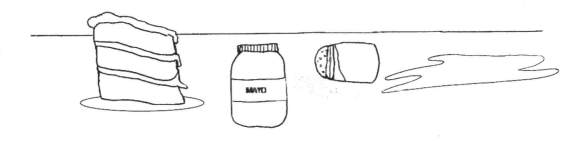

TROUTAPOTAMUS

The other day I saw the troutapotamus—
He lives in the water nearby.
I heard the sound of a thrash,
So I peeked through the grass and felt a splash,
And I saw him jump up and eat a fly!
He looked like he was half trout,
And the other half a hippopotamus.
He was big and round, and had slimy skin,
And I'm not telling another tall tale again,
But I'm sure he wants to remain anonymous!

THE END

There is nothing left but the sound of the wind.
Having no more than my thanks to send.
Everything I have right now has been penned.

Enclosed within these pages I hope you'll recommend!
Now you say you have read and grinned.
Don't know what else to say but…"The End!"

Index

Made in the USA
Monee, IL
14 May 2021